THE ADVANCING MAN

Living Life in Victory

ADEFIOYE SUNDAY ADEWUMI

SDX Publishing House (SDX Books)

THE ADVANCING MAN

Copyright © 2013
Adefioye Sunday Adewumi

All rights reserved.

No portion of this book may be used without the written permission of the publisher, with the exception of brief except in magazine articles, reviews, etc.

ISBN: 978-978-52464-0-7

Published in Nigeria by:
SDX Books
(Publishing subsidiary of Sadaxx Systems)

For further information or permission, please contact:
Adefioye Sunday Adewumi
Tel: (+234) 703-3985-337, (+234) 818-6948-268
sunday.adefioye@gmail.com

DEDICATION

I dedicate this book to God Almighty.

CONTENTS

Dedication

Contents

Introduction

Chapter 1:   In the Beginning

Chapter 2:   The Two Systems

Chapter 3:   The System of Fear

Chapter 4:   The Lots of Life

Chapter 5:   Time is Enough

Chapter 6:   The Fear of People

Chapter 7:   The God's System

Chapter 8:   Faith or Fear

Chapter 9:   Living the God's System

Chapter 10: The Place of the Holy Spirit

Chapter 11: The Word of God

Chapter 12: You can have all you need in life

Epilogue

Notes

About Author

INTRODUCTION

Every believer is to advance in life and live a life of victory. Everything that you need to live in the fullness of joy and advance confidently in the fulfillment of your purpose in life has been given to you in Christ Jesus. God is not interested in the suffering of His children. He is not interested in the stagnation, frustration and failures that many are passing through. He created you for the best. Everything He made is good.

In this world operated by a system of fear and turmoil, this book through the inspiration of the Holy Spirit presents biblical principles and guides to advance in life and walk over all life difficulties and challenges. You are to be a partaker of the divine nature of God and not partaker in the confusion of life. You are to live life in victory.

Great men who have imparted this world positively and have written their names on the sand of time are people who overcame the systems by which the world operates and confidently advances in the direction of their dreams and purpose. This world of unlimited possibilities and advancement is opened to everybody who operates the God's system. To advance in life you must believe that you can.

The only limitation to your advancement is your believe.

23 Jesus said unto him, If thou canst believe, all things are possible to him that believeth.
Mark 9:23(KJV)

God wants to see you advancing, excelling, prosperous, happy and in sound health. Your believe system and who, and what you believe greatly determines your lots in life. It is only believe in God that assures lasting success and victory.

Who we are and who we will become is largely the result of our believe. All the struggles of life is dependent on believe. Nobody has ever advanced in life without believe and purpose. If you know your root, and your root is God, you will manifest the abundant life that God wants you to live - life of purpose, fulfillment, and victory. Life of advancement and progress.

This book is structured in chapters, with the beginning chapter to give you insight into the original purpose of God for man. God does not create anyone without a purpose. Everyone who advances in life has a purpose and they know their purpose very well. The book also include chapters on overcoming the world systems of operation and living the God's system for victory in life. The concluding chapters of the book presents Godly steps to get everything you need in life as someone who is advancing in the direction of his purpose and fulfillment of his dreams.

To advance in life, you must have a dream, a purpose and a vision. Vision is what gives your life direction. Without a vision or purpose nobody advances in life.

Where there is no vision, the people perish . . .

Proverb 29:18 (KJV)

A man without a direction is like an anchorless ship. Drifting aimlessly about on the sea She has neither origin nor destination. Even if she has a destination, she cannot know when she get there.

Adefioye Sunday A.

I pray that this book by the inspiration of the Holy Spirit will help you overcome the struggles and frustration of life and transform you into wonder to behold, a miracle worker, an advancing man and advancing woman...

1
IN THE BEGINNING

Before God intervened, the beginning of the earth was dominated by confusion, stagnation and purposelessness (Gen 1:2).

And the earth was without form, and void; and darkness was upon the face of the deep...

Gen 1:2 (KJV)

And the Spirit of God moved upon the face of the waters. The Spirit could not do anything until God's will and desire was revealed and enforced through His word when He says "Let there be light". God does not create the darkness, He created light. God is not interest in the misfortune and frustration of His Children He is not interested in Stagnation. He did not create the earth without form, and void. He did not create an empty world of no progress. When God saw that the earth was stagnant, purposeless, and formless, He commanded "Let there be light"

"And God Said, Let there be light, and there was light."

Gen 1:3 (KJV)

When God speaks and the light manifest, He saw that it was GOOD and He separated the light from the darkness. Everything that God made was good. God is not the author of confusion. He is a good and working God

If you follow the account of creation from verse 1 to verse 25 in Genesis chapter 1, you will realise that everything that God made was good. And God made everything in the world first before He created man. Everything that man will need for survival and live abundantly are already available before his creation.

26 And God said, Let us make man in our image, after our likeness: and let them have dominion over the fish of the sea, and over the fowl of the air, and over the cattle, and over all the earth, and over every creeping thing that creepeth upon the earth.
27 So God created man in his own image, in the image of God created he him; male and female created he them.

28 And God blessed them, and God said unto them, Be fruitful, and multiply, and replenish the earth, and subdue it: and have dominion over the fish of the sea, and over the fowl of the air, and over every living thing that moveth upon the earth.

29 And God said, Behold, I have given you every herb bearing seed, which is upon the face of all the earth, and every tree, in the which is the fruit of a tree yielding seed; to you it shall be for meat.

30 And to every beast of the earth, and to every fowl of the air, and to every thing that creepeth upon the earth, wherein there is life, I have given every green herb for meat: and it was so.

Gen 1:26-30 (KJV)

God does not make any man without provision and vision. Before God created man, He first declared the vision and purpose for creating him. He says in verse 26, "Let us make man in our image, after our likeness: and let them have dominion over the fish of the sea, and over the fowl of the air . . . " This mean two things.

Firstly, no man is created without a purpose. You are created for a purpose. God does not do anything without a purpose. He established the purpose for creating man before he created him. You are not an accidental creation. Your existence is not a mistake. You have an important role to play in life. There are no two you. And you are uniquely created. One man that knows this truth very well was David. For he says;

"I will praise thee; for I am fearfully and wonderfully made: marvelous are thy works; and that my soul knoweth right well."

Psalm 139:14 (KJV)

This is one of the secrets of David, he knows his purpose and always appreciates God for it. You will also reign in life, if you discover your purpose and constantly acknowledge God for it. He knew he was special. He knew he was to reign as king. And he never doubted it. His knowledge of his purpose is not at face value "... and that my soul knoweth right well."

He knew within his soul that he is fearfully and wonderfully made. Then he acknowledged that God's works are marvelous! Friend, you are not just a man, you are not just a woman. You are not just anyone. You are a divine being with divine purpose here on earth.

Secondly, when God created man, he created him to have dominion over every situation of life. In verse 26 He says, "... and let them have dominion . . ." He does not create a helpless man. He does not create a beggarly man. He does not create a hopeless man. The man that God created is a man of purpose and authority. You are created with a purpose and you have the authority to fulfill that purpose here on earth.

When God created man, he created him in His own image and in His likeness He created him. What is the image of God?

"God is a Spirit: and they that worship Him must worship Him in spirit and in truth."

John 4:29

God is a Spirit; therefore, man is a spirit, being made in the image of God. And Jesus says in John 4:29 that whoever that wants to worship or contact God must worship and contact Him in spirit and in truth. You cannot contact or worship God with anything physical. When God created you, he breathe life into you, so you can become a living soul and a partaker of the divine nature (Gen2:7).

Sin and Our Redemption

When God made man, he gave him all the authority he needs to reign in life. When man sinned, the law came and he became bounded to the law. He lost his authority to the devil. Then death, frustration, confusion and turmoil of life came. The devil became the ruler of the world.

Because of God's love for man (John 3:16), He sends Christ to redeemed us from the curse of the law. Then Christ came and rescued us from the three curses of the law the curse of sickness, poverty and death. He gave us victory over the devil (I John 5:4-5).

13 Christ hath redeemed us from the curse of the law, being made a curse for us: for it is written, Cursed is every one that hangeth on a tree:
14 That the blessing of Abraham might come on the Gentiles through Jesus Christ; that we might receive the promise of the Spirit through faith.

Gal 3:13-14 (KJV)

Jesus did not only redeem us from the curse of the law, he also redeemed us back to our God (Rev 5:9), back to the divine nature of God. He restores us back to the original purpose for which God has made man. He restores us to a life of purpose, dominion and authority.

9 And they sung a new song, saying, Thou art worthy to take the book, and to open the seals thereof: for thou waist slain, and hast redeemed us to God by thy blood out of every kindred, and tongue, and people, and nation;
Rev 5:9 (KJV)

And finally, through his death and resurrection, he brings the blessings of Abraham to every nation (without any discrimination). And that we might receive the promise of the Spirit (of God) through faith. The gates are lifted, the mountains are leveled, the bars are broken and we are reconnected back to God by Jesus Christ and we can communicate with God with the help of the Holy Spirit.

Now you know that in the beginning, you are created for a purpose and you are given the authority to fulfill that purpose here on earth. You know that it is sin that causes separation between you and God and create a barrier between you and Him. You know that it is not God's will for you to suffer or live in poverty.

You know that frustration and stagnation is not the purpose of God for your life. God does not create darkness, He created light. God loves you and that is why he send His only son to die for you that you may be partaker in his divine kingdom.

16 For God so loved the world, that he gave his only begotten Son, that whosoever believeth in him should not perish, but have everlasting life.

John 3:16 (KJV)

Christ has redeemed you from the curse of frustration, stagnation, poverty, sickness, joblessness, death, and struggles. God still has those thoughts He had when He made you now. He still have you in mind (Jer 29:11). And with Him, your future is secured.

11 For I know the thoughts that I think toward you, saith the LORD, thoughts of peace, and not of evil, to give you an expected end.

Jer 29:11

(KJV)

Start seeing yourself in the image that God has created you. Clearly see that glorious future which God has pre-destinate you for.

5 Before I formed thee in the belly I knew thee; and before thou camest forth out of the womb I sanctified thee, and I ordained thee a prophet unto the nations.

Jer 1:5 (KJV)

Your Believe

There are two faces to life - the truth and the fact. The truth stands on God's Word while the fact stands on life's situations. David knew the truth, he always appreciates God. And that is why David said in Ps 139:14 that "... and that, my soul knoweth right well." He knew within his soul and spirit that he was wonderfully made. That is the truth. He knew who God created him to be and he lived a victorious life.

What do you believe? Do you believe the lies that the devil sows into your heart about your life? Do you believe the limiting thoughts about your future? Do you believe the names that people are calling you? Do you believe those gossips about you? Do you believe that your present situation or status quo cannot improve?

Do you believe that struggle always continues? David believe one thing, and this his soul knoweth right well. He believed that he is fearfully and wonderfully made. Meshach, Shadrach and Abednego believed one thing. They believe that their God is more than able to rescue and save them despite the life-and-death situation (Dan 3:16-18).

16 Shadrach, Meshach, and Abed-nego, answered and said to the king, O Nebuchadnezzar, we are not careful to answer thee in this matter.
17 If it be so, our God whom we serve is able to deliver us from the burning fiery furnace, and he will deliver us out of thine hand, O king.
18 But if not, be it known unto thee, O king, that we will not serve thy gods, nor worship the golden image which thou hast set up.

Dan 3:16-18 (KJV)

Daniel believed that the God that he serves can rescue him in the lion's den (Dan 6:1-23). The woman with the issue of blood believed that touching the hem of Jesus' garment will cure her ailment (Matt 9:20-22).

History is filled with people who believe in their purpose and by this believe, they have fulfilled their destiny and successfully written their names on the sand of time. Most of this people are not believers. If they can command great results, then we as believers can command greater results. Nelson Mandela believed that despite the hardships and imprisonment, he can save the blacks in South Africa. He became the first black President in South Africa. Thomas Edison believed that no matter how long it takes or how many times he tried and failed, and regardless of what people says, that he can make the incandescent bulb. He made the incandescent bulb.

The Wright brothers believed that it is possible for man to travel through air despite the claim by the people that they were crazy. They made the aircraft.

Abraham Lincoln believed that he can make a lasting impact on his generation regardless of the agony of losing his fiancé, failure in business and shameful defeat in elections. He became one of the most influential President of United States. These are men who believed in their purpose and vision in life.

In the beginning, God created man for a purpose, to be a co-creator, to make statements with our lives, to leave a legacy, to be a blessing, and to replenish the earth.

Many kings have died as slaves. Many boss died as servants. Many talents have been buried immature. Many destinies have faded away without fulfillment. Many rich men have died in poverty. WAKE UP! Your time is now! Take responsibilities where you are and believe God for where you are going.

See yourself as God sees you. Define yourself as who God says you are. Call yourself who God calls you. God called Abraham a Father of many nations, though he had no child, he is old and Sarah (his wife) have well pass menopause. He believed who God says he is. Even when he had only one son, and God told him to sacrifice Isaac, he went ahead without hesitation. He knew his God and believed Him as faithful. He believed that whether Isaac or no Isaac, he is a father of many nation. How it will come to pass does not concern him. He had peace and joy because God has spoken.

17 (As it is written, I have made thee a father of many nations,) before him whom he believed, even God, who quickeneth the dead, and calleth those things which be not as though they were.
18 Who against hope believed in hope, that he might become the father of many nations; according to that which was spoken, So shall thy seed be.

Rom 4:17-18 (KJV)

It is complete faith and trust in the Lord that brings about the manifestation of His promises. Have faith in God and believe in yourself, then you will be unstoppable. Believe that you can and you will!

You are born a champion. You are born a winner. Go about and start telling people the truth. Tell them who you are in Christ and not what circumstances says you are. Tell them you are blessed. Tell them you can get any job you desire. Tell them you are rich. Tell them you are to reign as king. Tell them the truth. The truth is what God says. The fact is what circumstance and men say. Refuse to be pitied. Refuse to be a beggar. Stand up for who you are. Rise up to your feet and look life straight in the eyes. Ignore the naysayers. Focus on your glorious destiny. Go and get that job. Rise and build that business. Study and be the best. Be a Champion! Be a Winner! Be a Blessing!

2
THE TWO SYSTEMS

There are two possible ways anyone can operate in life. Its either you are operating in God's system or you are operating the world's system. God's system says all things are possible. The world's system says that's crazy, nobody has ever done that before. God's system says you can have what you say. The world system says don't ask irrational or crazy requests and demands, that's impractical. God's system says the Lord shall provide all my needs according to His riches in glory. The World's system says let us sit and do feasibility studies. God system says cast thy net unto the sea. The world system says "I have been toiling and fishing all night to no avail." God system says walk on the sea. The world system says that's crazy, you will sink. God system says you are a father of many nations. World system says look at yourself, you are too old and your wife cannot ovulate.

THE WORLD'S SYSTEM

The world system is operated by the devil. That is why it is written that "Greater is he who lives in us (as believers) than he who lives in the world (devil) I John4:4. Christ cannot be greater than himself, but surely he is greater than the devil. And Christ lives in us (1Cor2:16).

The main aim of the devil is to misdirect us out of the way and system of God, hence to steal our joy. Everything in this world is operated by the world's system. Only the believers have risen above the operation of this world. The system of the world is a system of insecurities. It is a system of confusion and frustration. The devil and the world operate through fear. Fear leads to manipulations, deceptions, lies, worry, anxiety, and most of the negative feelings, actions and inactions. Fear operates in two ways - the desire to manipulate others or take advantage of others due to the fear that one has something to lose; and the incapacity to take informed actions due to worry or anxiety that something bad will happen. Fear is the result of extreme consciousness of our insecurities. As believers we are eternally secured in Christ.

The world system operates through fear. Fear causes insecurities, fear leads to lust. Fear paralyses us and breaks our ability to synchronize with the frequency of God. Fear blocks our reasoning and makes us receptive to devil. Fear makes a man to be a victim rather than victor.

3

THE SYSTEM OF FEAR

Fear Defined

Fear is broadly defined in the following ways;

1. Feeling of great worry or anxiety caused by the knowledge of danger. (Oxford English Dictionary)
2. A feeling of distress, apprehension, or alarm caused by impending danger, pain, etc.
3. To be afraid to do something or of a person or thing; dread
4. To feel anxiety about something
5. An emotion experienced in anticipation of some specific pain or danger (usually accompanied by a desire to flee or fight)

These are some of the definition of fear. The anatomy of fear composed of three things - a feeling, about the knowledge, and of an object. You can only be fearful of something you have its knowledge.

From the various definition, fear is the feeling of something that has not happened knowledge of danger, impending danger, afraid to do something, anxiety about something, and anticipation of.

All these are emotions that build up from events that has not occurred or not real. Fear really has no substance. Yet it is one of the reasons why many destiny and potentials are not being fully maximized. Fear of failure, fear of success, fear of what people will say, fear of what ifs, fear of death, fear of etc.

Fear is defined as False Evidence Appearing Real.
Joyce Meyer

A man who cannot conquer his fears, will never leave the ground.
Adefioye Sunday A.

Fear can be classified into two categories.
1. The fear of time, and
2. Fear of people.

THE FEAR OF TIME

The fear of time is magnified when today you brood about the past and worried or anxious about tomorrow. The fear of time is exhibited when you look at yourself, and begin to regret your past, or you look at your present situation and thinks hopelessly, or you look at the future and says "I can't make it". We always ask when? When? When? When will it happen? When will it come? When will I get there? When will I get the job? Many souls have been lost because of anxiety over "when". When you are afraid of time, your life will be in a rush. A life of rush opens you up to mistake and makes you vulnerable to satanic manipulations and frustrations. God is never in a rush. That is why He says in Habakuk 2:3, that though the vision and promise tarries, wait for it, it will surely come.

3 For the vision is yet for an appointed time, but at the end it shall speak, and not lie: though it tarry, wait for it; because it will surely come, it will not tarry.

Hab 2:2-3(KJV)

God always have a time for everything and God's time is always the best. Moses knew from a very young age that he is the deliverer of Israel. When he make attempt to fulfill his destiny (at a wrong time), his own people are the ones that exposed and betrayed him. He had to run for his life (Exo 2:14-15). And the deliverer of a great nation became a shepherd, leading and delivering sheep and lambs in the jungle (Exo 3:1). But without the training that Moses undergoes tendering sheep, he would not have qualified as the deliverer of Israel. There is always a God's time.

14 And he said, Who made thee a prince and a judge over us? intendest thou to kill me, as thou killedst the Egyptian? And Moses feared, and said, Surely this thing is known.
15 Now when Pharaoh heard this thing, he sought to slay Moses . But Moses fled from the face of Pharaoh, and dwelt in the land of Midian: and he sat down by a well.
Exodus 2:14-15(KJV)

3:1 Now Moses kept the flock of Jethro his father in law, the priest of Midian: and he led the flock to the backside of the desert, and came to the mountain of God, even to Horeb.   *Exodus 3:1(KJV)*

Joseph knew that he has a bright future (Gen 37). But until he passed all trials and undergoes necessary training as a slave and as a prisoner. He was not qualified to be a prime minister in Egypt. This does not mean you should be passive and not do anything. God's time only answers to people who are prepared for it. Moses did not sit down waiting for God's time. He was working and working hard because in the concluding part of Exodus 3:1, "and (Moses) came to the mountain of God, even (as far as) to Horeb". Joseph was diligent in his work that is why his Master promoted him to be the head of his household. You have to be diligent in whatever you are doing. But you don't have to be in haste.

29 Seest thou a man diligent in his business? he shall stand before kings; he shall not stand before mean men.
                                         Proverb 22:29(KJV)

It is your responsibility to do your best and leave the rest to God. Your job is to plant the seed of hard work, and let God bring the increase in His time.

6 I have planted, Apollo watered; but God gave the increase.   *1 Cor 3:6 (KJV)*

It is ignorance that makes men rush into things. It is lack of knowledge that makes us to be so much in haste that we ignore the promises and vision of God for our lives. Abraham was hastened out of God's timing when he listened to Sarah to have sexual intercourse with his servant. Many people have rushed through life and met with unexpected end because they are not in synchrony with God's timing.

8 But, beloved, be not ignorant of this one thing, that one day is with the Lord as a thousand years, and a thousand years as one day.
9 The Lord is not slack concerning his promise, as some men count slackness; but is longsuffering to us-ward, not willing that any should perish, but that all should come to repentance.   *2 Peter 3:8-9(KJV)*

Life without proper timing is a clumsy life. There is a natural order in which things follow. God does not create man before other things for a purpose. God does not create the fishes before the water. God does not create day and night before he said let there be light.

Everything in life have a divine arrangement. God does not create the grass, the herb yielding seed, and the tree yielding fruits before he created dry land rarth. He does not create any living creature until He has created where they will live and what they will eat. God has not made any man without adequate and enough provision for him to live abundantly here on earth. God has a timing and a divine order in which He unfolds His plans and purposes. Everything you ever need in this life has been created. It exists somewhere.

Men are in sizes; and Life is in Stages.
Bishop David O Oyedepo

It is only people with devilish intentions that will want to rush you into things. When you encounter such people, slow down, meditate on God's word, and rethink about any step or decision you are about to take. Nothing good has ever come or manifested in a hurry. There is always a process.

In the world system, you are in a hurry and rush because you are afraid of something. Fear is the root of all rush in life. You are afraid you will loose your job. You are afraid you will loose a customer. You are afraid you will loose the contact. You are afraid you will not meet up the schedule. You are afraid you will loose your money. You are afraid of everything that makes you to rush in anyway.

When you lack control over your time, you lack control of yourself. When you lack control of yourself, you will invariably lack control over your life. Meaning one way or the other, someone or something else is in control of you. And this defeats the divine purpose of God for your life. When you are under control of the natural world, you live a lowly and defeated life.

Time can be defined as a fragment of eternity.
Pastor E. A. Adeboye

To conquer the fear of timing, you must know that time is only a resource that must be well managed. Time is like money. The value and satisfaction you derived from money is more important than the amount of the money. How you use your time is more important than how much time you have.

Quality is better than quantity. Your time is your responsibility. Every man on earth is given the same amount of time every day. How you use your time and what you achieve in relation to the satisfaction and fulfillment you derived from your results is what makes the difference.

Time is not to be spent, it is to be invested
Bishop David O. Oyedepo

To live a happy and stress-free life, you need to conquer your fear of time. To conquer the fear of time you should understand that yesterday is gone, today is yours and tomorrow will come. So do your best today, never leave till tomorrow what you can do today. When tomorrow comes it will surely come with its own responsibilities.

Many people go through life, carrying on their head loads that are meant for five years to come. You only have the energy and resource to solve today's problems today. That is why when Jesus teaches his disciples how to pray, he requested that God should give us our daily bread.

To advance in life, you must conquer your fear of time. To live a dominion life, you must understand God's timing. Your understanding of how time works in the kingdom is what sets you apart from the pack. That is what releases you from the rush of life.

When you are released from the rush of life, you are totally free and you experience what Jesus called "Peace that surpass understanding" and "Joy unspeakable".

Sometimes when you do something that is in congruence with your true nature with the nature of God in you, you feel elated, you are happy from within.

Understanding and conquering the fear of time does not make you irresponsible. It makes you more responsible. When you conquer the fear of time, you begin to see every event in your life in a newer perspective. There is a paradigm shift in your reasoning about life. You begin to meet deadlines. You keep to time. You meet appointments. And you deliver on time. You do everything you have to do in smooth order. You transit from one responsibility to the other without any hitches.

LEARN TO SAY NO

Many people in life only carry loads that are about 5% useful to them. The remaining 95% are loads imposed on them by other people. You cannot achieve success until you learn to say no to many things in life.

The advancing man advances confidently in the direction of his dreams.

Most times the best word to say is No. To achieve maximum fulfillment of your destiny, you should learn to say no to things that loads and brings burden upon you unnecessary without adding much or any value to life or any value to any ones' life. You have a purpose. Many people have been lured and distracted from their purpose by the various carefully devised means of manipulations.

Remember, you are unique. The advancing man is always focused. He keeps his face to the sunshine and he cannot see the shadows. He does not look left nor look right. He does not stagger with his convictions about his mission. He looks straight at life in the eyes and says NO to the distractions of life. He doesn't listen to side-talks nor look at the fancy alluring things of life. Just as no is the best word to say, it is also sometimes the most difficult word to say.

He is a man indeed, the man that can look at life straight in the eyes and say NO.
Adefioye Sunday A

4
THE LOTS OF LIFE

Before Abraham can fully receive the promises of God, he had to say NO to Lot. Lot can be a lot of things in life. Lot can even be some of your close friends. Lot can be those things that you enjoy doing. Abraham's blessing does not fully manifest until he get rid of Lot. Lot was Abraham's close family. However, their intimate relationship is bringing yoke upon Abraham and causing delay in the manifestation of God's blessing in his life.

Strife between Abraham and Lot

5 And Lot also, which went with Abram, had flocks, and herds, and tents.
6 And the land was not able to bear them, that they might dwell together: for their substance was great, so that they could not dwell together.

7 And there was a strife between the herdmen of Abram's cattle and the herdmen of Lot's cattle: and the Canaanite and the Perizzite dwelled then in the land.

Gen 13:5-7(KJV)

When you are carrying a lot of unnecessary load on your road to fulfill destiny, there will always be a strife and conflict of purpose. There will always be situation of yoke, frustration and confusion. God is not a man, so He cannot lie. He has blessed you and pre-destinate you for a purpose. The blessing and his promises will surely come. Verse 5 of Genesis 15 can be interpreted as And Lot also (or even Lot), which (because he) went with Abram, had flocks, and herds, and tents. This means Lot was blessed because of his relationship with Abraham. He was blessed because he walked with a blessed man. However, there was confusion and conflict of purpose.

When the weeds grows, un-removed, with the seed.
It grows to a point that it begins to choke the seed.
Adefioye Sunday A

Many things we do in life are like weeds. They are of no value and bring no fruit. We waste our time on lot of things that defeats our purpose in life. Lot was like the weed, that thrives on the seed and when he grows to a level, it begins to choke the seed. Many destinies have been choked to death because of lack of understanding and the inability to say NO to the lots of life. Many people are frustrated, confused and live in poverty not because they are not brilliant or talented. They remain helpless in their situations because they cannot say NO to many things in their lives. They cannot look at the Lots and declare liberation.

You should begin to see your glorious destiny. Begin to clearly visualize your purpose here on earth. Rise up and say NO to the LOTS of life that are bringing yoke and burden on you. You don't have to crawl through life on your palms and knees when you are to be driving the best car and live the best life.

History is filled with people who are once rich in a godly way and died poor and wretched. On their journey, they carry a lot of lots. And the lot of lots choked and destroys their lots in life.

You have to be spiritually alert and build your inner strength and ability to say NO. I am not saying you should not help people. Help people with spiritual sensitivity and wisdom. Some people are like weeds which you have to watch out for. Many things you have you don't need. Many friends you have are not necessary. Friends are to be carefully selected. And you have to be spiritually sensitive to any friend you choose. You will always have this "aura" and feeling of an envisioned future with your friends' picture in it. You will always know if you have the right friend.

Learn to associate with people who are going somewhere with their lives. People who are visionaries, who plans ahead and thinks both in the short-term and long-term - Success is contagious!

14 Be ye not unequally yoked together with unbelievers: for what fellowship hath righteousness with unrighteousness? and what communion hath light with darkness?

2 Cor 6:14(KJV)

To advance in life, you have to say NO to the lots of life. Check within you if whatever you are about to do or are doing is from within your heart. Are you having fulfillment and peace within you about whatever you are doing or about to do? Always check yourself and measure yourself on the scale of the Word of God, to ascertain if you are in congruence with the will of God.

The Lot that Abraham went out with causes confusion and delay in the manifestation of his blessings. God is not the author of confusion (1 Cor 14:33).

Separation between Abraham and Lot

8 And Abram said unto Lot, Let there be no strife, I pray thee, between me and thee, and between my herdmen and thy herdmen; for we be brethren.
9 Is not the whole land before thee? separate thyself, I pray thee, from me: if thou wilt take the left hand,
Then I will go to the right; or if thou depart to the right hand, then I will go to the left.

Gen 13:8-9(KJV)

Just as Abraham took that bold step and say NO to Lot. To advance into your next levels, you have to say NO to the Lots in your life. It doesn't have to be friends only. It may be a job, if you are not been fulfilled and are given inner guide to a peaceful direction. It can even be your family (not to ignore or neglect them) separation is not segregation or denial. But anything that brings you yoke, frustration and drags you down is a lot in your life. Anything that does not add value to your life or does not have the potential to help in the fulfillment of your destiny is lot in your life. Anything that can cause distraction or divert you out of your purpose is lot in your life. Even people's opinion or words that are intended to manipulate or distract you is lot that you must say NO to.

Before Abraham's blessing could fully come, he got rid of Lot. He said NO to Lot. He said NO to confusion. He said NO to strife. He said NO to Yoke. You must also constantly take that step to fulfill your purpose in life and to open the door for the manifestation of your blessings.

Abraham Blessed After Lot has Left

14 And the LORD said unto Abram, after that Lot was separated from him, Lift up now thine eyes, and look from the place where thou art northward, and southward, and eastward, and westward:

15 For all the land which thou seest, to thee will I give it, and to thy seed for ever.

16 And I will make thy seed as the dust of the earth: so that if a man can number the dust of the earth, then shall thy seed also be numbered.

17 Arise, walk through the land in the length of it and in the breadth of it; for I will give it unto thee.

Gen 13:14-17(KJV)

After Lot had separated from Abraham, God spoke and He bestow abundant and generational blessings upon Abraham. Note that this does not happen when Lot was with Abraham. Though they were blessed but Lot is limiting God's favour over Abraham. Your blessing is around the corner, your abundance is certain, your prosperity is sure, but you have to get rid of the lots before it can fully manifest.

Many things and many people are time wasters. Things that we do in life can be categorized into two – things that are Urgent and things that are Important.

These can be further classified as things that are;
    i.   Urgent and Not Important
    ii.   Not Urgent and Important
    iii.   Not Urgent and Not Important
    iv.   Urgent and Important

To be productive in life, you need to constantly work on things that are important and get rid of things that are not important. You do things that are urgent and important first before things that are not urgent and important.

Weigh your activities during the day. How much energy and time are you wasting on things that are not important? Some calls are not important. Chatting during working hours is not important. Gossips are the most unreasonable activities that occupied most of peoples time. Some addiction, worry and anxiety are like it. It chokes your health and you achieve nothing from indulging in them.

Things that are important add value to you and make you feel accomplished. Investing time in prayer and study of the Word is important. Quality relationships building are important. Study and making plans are important, initiating sales calls is important. Spending time with a big customer or potential client is important. Important things are the things that help you to be a better you in life. They are the things that help you to accomplish your dreams in life.

Things that are not important sap your energy and reduce you to nothing. Learn to constantly say NO to things that are not important. And say NO to the lots of life. Concentrate your energy on things that are important and are taking you to the direction of your purpose in life.

Time management is life management. Failure to manage time is life failure, because life is measured within frame of time. Wasting time is damaging life. Don't expose your life to time wasters because they are life damagers. Life is allotted in time frames. Allowing time to pass is allowing life to pass.
Bishop David Abioye

5
TIME IS ENOUGH

All the Time is Yours, Understanding is all you need

Every day, God gave everyone 24 hours each. Equal amount of time, equal amount of opportunities. Whatever you do with your time is your responsibility. Whether you use your time wisely or not, time will always go.

Time and tide wait for nobody.

Anonymous

Your time is yours and my time is mine. But only the wise knows that time is not to be spent, time is to be invested. And like every investment, the result and what you accomplish is the evidence.

When you spend your time, the time is gone and you have no result. When you invest your time, the time is gone but you have results.

The distinction between people who accomplished great things in life and people who crawl beggarly through life is that accomplished people always invest their time while poor and unaccomplished people spend their time. Whether you spend or invest your time, your time is always yours.

You need to understand the system of timing before you can advance in life. Everything has a time. And your time is always yours. If you can see the truth of this statement clearly, your life will be filled with serene and peaceful experiences. You sleep at night like every other people because the night time has come. You wake in the morning like everyone else because the day has broken. You go through the day like every other people. The only difference is the result which serves as certificate for what you have invested your time in. While some are busy making meaning out of life, others are busy wasting away their time.

Whether you are investing your time, busy utilizing your time to bring God's promise to pass in your life, or you are spending your time playing games, gisting, gossiping, chatting and waiting (doing nothing) for the right time for God to manifest, all the time is yours and equal amount of time is given to all. You are completely responsible for what you do with your time.

Only people, who have vision in life, constantly seize time and work towards the fulfillment of destiny can manifest God's glory and reign as kings in life. No blessing is accidental. You have all the time to fulfill your glorious destiny in life. Nobody has ever been blessed without preparation. Every blessing in life is a connection between preparation and opportunity. You have all the time you need to prepare. Moses had to work (as a shepherd for a long time) before he qualified to deliver Israel.

Isaac had to sow before he could reap a hundredfold in the same year, though he inherited the blessings of Abraham.

Everything that Abraham had was destroyed and the wells were covered up by the Philistines (Gen 26:15). This should give Isaac a hopelessness mentality. But Isaac was a working man, he sowed in the land. And that is what makes him qualify for the hundred fold increase and the blessings that follow. Verse 13 says that he waxed great, and went forward, and grew until he became very great.

Something that is not active cannot wax and there is no forward movement without a movement or an action. Growth is a function of purposeful actions. Without quality use of his time working to bring God's blessing to pass, he cannot waxed great, go forward and grow until he became VERY great.

12 Then Isaac sowed in that land, and received in the same year an hundredfold: and the LORD blessed him.
13 And the man waxed great, and went forward, and grew until he became very great:
14 For he had possession of flocks, and possessions of herds, and great store of servants: and the Philistines envied him.

Gen 26:12-14(KJV)

The other part of that story is the side of the Philistines. They were living in the same land as Isaac. They have equal amount of time. In fact they are exposed to equal opportunity. However, while Isaac was sowing, they became envious. Remember, all the time is yours and understanding is all you need.

What you do with your time is your responsibility. God's promise always answers to time. But to receive his promise, you have to be prepared - sow and invest your time in productive activities. When Jesus called Peter and Andrew, they were working diligently. They were fishers (or fisher men). They invested their time in productive activity. This is one of the things that make them qualify to be disciples of Jesus.

18 And Jesus, walking by the sea of Galilee, saw two brethren, Simon called Peter, and Andrew his brother, casting a net into the sea: for they were fishers.
19 And he saith unto them, Follow me, and I will make you fishers of men.

Matt 4:18-19(KJV)

Your present situation is not an excuse. Your present condition is not a limitation. Your education is not a barrier. The only limitation is your believe, is in your mind. It is whether you have a vision or not. Peter was toiling all night working when majority of his colleagues are sleeping. He was prepared as a fisher to qualify as fisher of men. What you have today is enough for you to start. You can start right where you are.

When Christ called James and John, they were in the middle of an activity, they were not dormant, they were in the ship mending their nets. And verse 20 of Mark 1 says, "And straightaway, he (Jesus) called them." Mark 1:19-20.

Mathew (Levi) was sitting at the tax (custom) office when Christ called him. He was a tax (custom) officer before he could qualify as a disciple of Christ. Mark 2:24.

Paul was a hardworking man. His academic qualification and strong intellectual ability prepare him for the great assignment that God gave him. He was aggressive and constantly moving. He was on a journey when Christ met him. This gave him the necessary perseverance and understanding to withstand the challenges on his quest to fulfill his purpose as a minister of the gospel. He ends up writing most of the epistles in the New Testament.

3 And as he journeyed, he came near Damascus: and suddenly there shined round about him a light from heaven:
4 And he fell to the earth, and heard a voice saying unto him, Saul, Saul, why persecutest thou me?

Acts 9:3-4(KJV)

All the time you have today is to prepare you for tomorrow. How well you use today will determine the quality of life you live tomorrow. Tomorrow cannot come until today is gone. What you accomplish today is your certificate for passing through today. What certificate do you have when the night time come?

Your understanding of the concept of time is your key to conquer time and to seize time as a tool and not bondage to open the doors for the manifestation of God's blessing in your life. You don't have to be afraid of whether your time has gone or it is too early. The best time is now. God works in the present. God's time is NOW.

You are not dancing like a puppet to the strings hold by the world. You are advancing confidently in the direction which God has purported for you. Whether you do something or you do nothing, time will always go. You are not in a hurry and neither are you in a rush. You are not stagnant and purposeless. You are constantly moving forward. Get up and do something, time is enough for you to begin. You are an advancing man. You are advancing woman. Go and fulfill your destiny.

6
FEAR OF PEOPLE

Many people have been paralyzed largely because of either what people tell them, what people will say or do. Working and dealing with people requires divine wisdom. And wisdom alone is not enough, you should also get understanding.

7 Wisdom is the principal thing; therefore get wisdom: and with all thy getting get understanding.
8 Exalt her, and she shall promote thee: she shall bring thee to honour, when thou dost embrace her.

Prov 4:7-8(KJV)

How well you can understand people, and conquer your fear of people, will largely determine how far you can go in life because you must meet people. You must interact with people. You need people to survive. Man is a social being.

Our co-existence as humans is what has brought about the modern civilization and essentially has sustained the human race. No one can survive in this world alone. To thrive in this world require wisdom to which to understand and deal with people.

The first type of fear that paralyzes many to advance in life is the fear of what people will say. A life that depends on what people will say is a life of stagnation. Nobody can move forward in life until he conquers the fear of what people will say. Whether you are very rich or you are living in abject poverty, people will always have something to say about you. Whether you have 5 cars or you have 0 cars, people will surely have something to say about you. Whether you fail or you succeed, people will find something to talk about you. When I started my first business in 2012 and was passing through some challenges, it was some of my family members that first mocked me. It was the people that are closest to me that first belittle my dreams.

It is always pathetic that people with bright potentials suddenly give up on their dreams because of what some people who doesn't know what they are doing does to them or people who doesn't know what they are saying says.

People's opinion is always their own opinion, and it is personal to them. Some people may be under the influence of alcohol, then they talk negatively to you, and you let that affect you. Some other people may have deformed personality, and you let what they will do or does affect you.

Nothing in this world can affect you until you permit it. Nobody can hurt you until you allow it. You have absolute power over how you react to how people treat or will treat you in life.

You must understand that you don't have control over what people say. You don't have control over what other people does. You can only control how you allow what people say or does to affect you.

When you live by what people say or what people will say, you don't have a life of your own. You are not created by peoples' opinion. You are created by the Almighty God and for a divine purpose. Who does not create you does not have any power over you. An advancing man does not care about what people will say. In fact he thrives on the realization that people will always talk about him. Stop living your life hiding because of what people will say.

Get out! Go and get that job. Get up! Build that business. Stand tall! Be bold! And move confidently in the direction of your dreams.

The sweetest part of life is when you achieve those things which people say you cannot achieve.
Anonymous

If you must grow in life, people must talk about you. If Noah had listened to the people or fear what people will say, he will not have built the ark. If he was afraid that people will think that he was crazy, he will not have successfully built the ark.

God's opinion is His Word. God's opinion is superior to people's opinion. What God said about you is greater than what people say about you. If God approves you, you don't need the approval of men. God's verdict over your life and purpose is the final. You have a divine mandate!

When God speaks to Jeremiah, he was fearful of what people will say of him as a small child, he complained. But God does not care about what people think or says. He is no respecter of man. He sent forth His words and His word manifested.

6 Then said I, Ah, Lord GOD! behold, I cannot speak: for I am a child.7 But the LORD said unto me, Say not, I am a child: for thou shalt go to all that I shall send thee, and whatsoever I command thee thou shalt speak.
8 Be not afraid of their faces: for I am with thee to deliver thee, saith the LORD.

Jer 1:4-8(KJV)

When God speaks, He put everything in place to make His word come to pass. God is perfect in all things. He will never say something he cannot do. And there is nothing He said that shall not manifest. He said that His thought towards you are good and not of evil that you shall have an expected end (Jer 29:11).

11 For I know the thoughts that I think toward you, saith the LORD, thoughts of peace, and not of evil, to give you an expected end.

Jer 29:11 (KJV)

If God says that His thought towards you is of peace, good and not of evil, and He said this He did to give you an expected end. Then what type of end are you expecting? Are you expecting the end suggested by people's opinion or the end that God declared? If God says His thought towards you is of peace, then who's thought on earth should affect you? God's Word is the final. His Word is the ultimate verdict for your life.

8:1 There is therefore now no condemnation to them which are in Christ Jesus, who walk not after the flesh, but after the Spirit.   *Rom 8:1(KJV)*

In the New Testament, Romans 8:1 tells us that nobody (regardless of position and age) can condemn us as a believer who is walking diligently in the light of God. Why? Because, if God be for us, nobody can be against us (Rom 8:31)

31 What shall we then say to these things? If God be for us, who can be against us?   *Rom 8:31(KJV)*

33 Who shall lay anything to the charge of God's elect? It is God that justifieth.   *Rom 8:33(KJV)*

It has been clearly stated that nobody can lay a charge against you once you are walking according to the will of God. You are God's elect. You must rise above the negative opinion of people and put on the cloth of God's righteousness.

As an advancing man, you are not held captive by what people will say or do. You are backed up by a capable God and you are ultimately empowered by Him. Shake yourself up. Cheer yourself up. Lighten up. Turn your ears and eyes to only what God says and promised.

People's (negative and limiting) opinions have no substance. In fact what people do to you or will do to you is insignificant when you know the kind of God that is behind you. The same people that praise you today will come and mock you tomorrow. People who mock you today will come and praise you tomorrow. Even Jesus was not spared from the unstable character of men. The same people that praised him on his entrance into Jerusalem shouted that he should be crucified. He was mocked by his own people, and betrayed by someone closest to him.

For you to advance in life, you must conquer your fear of what people will say or do to you. When God created you, He breathed life into you and created you in His own image - Spirit. You have in you the Spirit of life, of power and of confidence.

7 For God hath not given us the spirit of fear; but of power, and of love, and of a sound mind.

2 Tim 1:7(KJV)

The real you is powerful beyond measure. The real you is the spirit man. The spirit that God gave you is not timid, he is not fearful. He is a spirit of (unlimited) power, a spirit of love and a spirit of completely sound mind, health and self control. And that is who you are, regardless of what anybody thinks or says. God has defined you.

People will try to define you. They will try to define everything you do. But God have a heavenly definition for who you are. He has defined you according to His Word. How do you define yourself?

You can only rise to the level at which you rise above what people think or will think, what people does or will do, and what people say or will say. You can only achieve as far as you think you can. The only limitation is you. Your vision is for you. Your purpose is uniquely for you.

Rise above limiting believes and negative opinions of people. There is a saying that "the sky is the limit". For an advancing man, the sky is the beginning. And the sky is far above any man. That is where to start. Go and get what is yours. If you know what you want, if you know what you desire, if you know what you worth, then go out and get it.

Define yourself according to who God says you are. Declare your future according to what God says it is. Stop limiting yourself. And all the best is yours.

7
THE GOD'S SYSTEM

God have a mode of operation. God is an unchangeable God. His mode of operation is the same as at the time of creation as it is today. Only the people that live by God's mudus-operandi reign as kings in life. The only key that unlocks the supernatural here on earth is FAITH. God operates by FAITH. Everything in God's kingdom manifests by Faith. It is by Faith that everything in heaven and on earth are created by the Word of God.

1 In the beginning was the Word, and the Word was with God, and the Word was God.
2 The same was in the beginning with God.
3 All things were made by him; and without him was not any thing made that was made.
John 1:1-3(KJV)

3 Through faith we understand that the worlds were framed by the word of God, so that things which are seen were not made of things which do appear.

Heb 11:3(KJV)

In this world dominated by fear, only faith can make you live an exceptional life. A man without faith is dead while alive. Nobody can advance in life without faith. Nobody can reign in life without faith. Faith is the key to everything in life

God's system is a system of Faith. Throughout the earthly days of Christ he operated the God's system the system of Faith. As an advancing man, you need faith at every step and stage on your way to fulfill destiny. Faith is the key. Faith is the answer. Faith is the power that unlocks doors of possibilities. A life of faith is a life of unlimited possibilities. Nothing can stop a man of faith.

What is Faith is Not

Faith is not a force.

Faith is not a strategy.

Faith is not a secret.

Faith is not magic.

Faith is not metaphysics.

Faith is not mind reading.

Faith is not sorcery.

But faith is,

11:1 Now faith is the substance of things hoped for, the evidence of things not seen.   *Heb 11:1(KJV)*

    The kingdom faith is the absolute believe and Strong conviction that you have what you expect or asked. You live like it, you talk like it. The kingdom faith is explained when Paul said in Romans that God is the one who quickeneth the dead, and called those things which be not as though they were.

17 (As it is written, I have made thee a father of many nations,) before him whom he believed, even God, who quickeneth the dead, and calleth those things which be not as though they were.

                                                 Rom 4:17(KJV)

Remember that;

1. Before God created man, he created everything on earth.
2. Before he created the fishes, he created the waters
3. Before he created every other animal on land, he created the land, grasses, trees and everything necessary for their survival.

Therefore, everything you ever need already exists. All you need is to apply faith and claim it. Every destiny already has all necessary things for its fulfillment. An advancing man is a man full of faith. A man of faith walk in the realization and reality that he has everything he ever needed.

When God make a promise, the promise is fulfilled at the instance. Your responsibility is to apply faith to receive what God promised. Without faith nobody can receive anything from God. Faith is defined in Hebrew 11:1, as the substance of things hoped for, and evidence of things not seen.

Another word for substance is material or anything physical that can be touched, seen or felt. Substance of things is reality or core of the thing. As it is used in that definition, substance is synonymous to "physical manifestation". Hope simply means anticipation or expectance. When you hope for a thing, you are expecting that thing. You are anticipating its manifestation or arrival. Faith is not hope and hope is not faith.

The second part of that definition of faith says that faith is the evidence of things not seen. Some synonyms for the word evidence are proof, facts, confirmation, authentication and verification. Therefore, I rephrase the second part in the definition of faith as "the proof, confirmation, authentication and verification of the things not seen.

To sum the two parts together, faith is therefore; "the physical manifestation and reality of the things expected, and the proof, confirmation, authentication and verification of things that are not seen, touched or felt."

Faith is not hope and hope is not faith

Faith says I have what I say.

Hope says I should have what I say.

Faith says all things are possible.

Hope says all things may be possible.

Faith says I am a winner. Hope says I may win.

Faith is not hope and hope is not faith.

Faith is present. Hope is future.

Faith answers NOW. Hope answers later.

Hope is one of the compositions of faith. Faith is not faith without hope. But Faith is greater than hope. Hope has no substance. Hope has no evidence. Hope is abstract, only an expectation and anticipation of things expected. Hope is the oil that drives faith. But faith always stands where hope fails.

Many people operate in hope when they think they are operating in faith. When you are in hope, you are still expecting. When you are operating in faith, you receive. When you are in faith your feelings, actions, speech, and thoughts aligns with the reality of your desire. You live it.

The disciples of Christ received power in Matt 10:1 but they couldn't do anything with it. Faith goes hand in hand with strong believe and unyielding conviction that you have what you say.

10:1 And when he had called unto him his twelve disciples, he gave them power against unclean spirits, to cast them out, and to heal all manner of sickness and all manner of disease.

Matt 10:1(KJV)

In Matthew 17, the same disciples whom Christ gave power could not do anything with what they have. The fact that they could not cast the devil out of the boy does not mean they do not have the power. They have it at the instance that Jesus Christ gave it to them. Many kings have died as slaves because they cannot see themselves as kings. Because they died as slaves does not mean they are not king. They are because God predestinate them to be. Many potential have been buried with their carrier unfulfilled because the carrier is blind to the fact that they have it - weak in faith.

Many people have risen from hopeless situation to become great in life. You can have a car and still be begging for ride. You can be a billionaire and still be looking for penny around. What you belief is what you receive. And you receive what you believe by faith.

Believe without faith is a wish. Faith without believe is fake.
Adefioye Sunday A

It is faith that transforms what you believe into its physical equivalent. Jesus Christ cast out the devil out of the boy in Matt chapter 17, not only because he is the son of God. He cast out the devil because he is faith personified. He is the author and finisher of our faith (Heb 12:2). He bestowed upon us the same power and authority as believers. In fact he says we shall do works and deeds that are greater than he did (John 14:12). But the disciples could not cast out the evil spirit just as many believers finds it difficult to cast out poverty, cast out joblessness, cast out sickness, cast out depression, cast out challenges of life.

The fact that the disciples could not cast out the demon because of their unbelief, does not mean they don't have the power. And Jesus gave a remedy for unbelief. The only remedy for unbelief is faith.

19 Then came the disciples to Jesus apart, and said, Why could not we cast him out?
20 And Jesus said unto them, Because of your unbelief...
Matt 17:19-20(KJV)

He said, the disciples could not cast out the evil spirit "because of their unbelief" - unbelief in what? Unbelief in the fact that they have power against all unclean spirits to cast them out, to heal all manner of sickness and all manner of disease (Matt 10:1).

In the same way, many people don't believe that prosperity is their heritage (2 John 2, Gal 3:14; 2Cor8:9), hence, they live all their lives in poverty.

Many don't believe that divine health is theirs and that they were healed from all manner of sicknesses and diseases (Isa 53:5, Matt 8:17).

Many are barren in life because they don't believe that God does not create anyone to be barren, He wants us to be fruitful (Gen 1:28, Exo 23:26).

Many live in lack because they do not believe that they have the right to live in abundance (Ps 23:1, Eph 3:20). What do you believe? Whatever God says you have, you have. If God says you are rich, then you are rich. If God says you cannot be barren, then you are not barren.

The level of your believe and what you believe greatly determines the type of life you live on earth.
Adefioye Sunday A

Faith is the only key to unlimited maximization of potentials. People who advance in life, are men of great faith. People who have greatly impact our lives are men of great faith. They are men who believed in who they are. They believe in their potentials. They believe in their talents. They believe in their vision. They believe in their destiny. And above all, they have the faith to diligently pursue their goals and persist in the face of challenges.

In the race of life, Men of faith are Unstoppable.

Adefioye Sunday A

God is not partial he gave everyone a measure of faith (Rom 12:3). Therefore, you don't pray for faith. It is already in you. To advance in life, you must awake to this reality. You must believe that you have all the power to transform your life into wonders within you. You don't need a gigantic faith to move a mountain. What Christ said is;

*...... For verily I say unto you, If ye have faith as a **GRAIN OF MUSTARD SEED**, ye shall say unto this mountain, Remove hence to yonder place; and it shall remove; and nothing shall be impossible unto you.*

Matt 17:20(KJV)

With faith as small as mustard seed, Christ said, "Nothing shall be impossible unto you". The world system through fear, intimidation and manipulations wants you to live a defeated life. But in God's system you are to live a victorious and kingly life through faith.

No King can reign for long in life without the believe and faith that he is the King.
Adefioye Sunday A

Men of faith are like a moving train. Moving confidently in the direction of their destination. Nothing can stop them until they reach their destination.
Adefioye Sunday A

Godly Faith Works in Love

The God kind of faith is a faith that works in love. Faith in the God's system is propelled by love - love towards God and man.

6 For in Jesus Christ neither circumcision availeth any thing, nor uncircumcision; but faith which worketh by love. *Gal 5:6 (KJV)*

When your faith is charged by love, you operate in the realm of God for God is love (1John 4:8, 16). To live successfully in the God system, you need to live in the true nature of God which is love.

16 And we have known and believed the love that God hath to us. God is love; and he that dwelleth in love dwelleth in God, and God in him.

1John 4:16 (KJV)

Love eliminates all fears and insecurities - it defeats the world system of operation .It is the key to the highest kind of faith.

8
FAITH OR FEAR

The opposite of faith is fear. Faith and fear cannot co-exist. Where there is faith, fear disappears. Fear signifies a lack of faith. Fear is the most dangerous trap of destiny the devil has ever invented. Fear of failure. Fear of success. Fear of people. Fear of sicknesses. A life of fear is a life of defeat. People who walk in fear are always defeated in life.

Fear paralyses your reason. Fear shuts you out of God's will. Fear destroys your creativity. Fear kills your initiative. Fear of today, fear of tomorrow. It is fear that makes people hopeless. Men of fear achieve nothing in life. And men of fear are the greatest problem and menace of life. Nothing is possible for that man whom fear dominates.

Destroy fear and you will be opened to a new world of possibilities. Conquer fear and you will be unstoppable.

The advancing man has conquered fear. He is fearless. He has master to transform fear to faith. He constantly charges forward. Walking over fear and destroying all strongholds.

The one who advances in life, is the one who has conquered fear.
Adefioye Sunday A

As I said earlier, fear has no substance. Faith is all you need to advance in life. Faith in God. Faith in yourself. Faith in your future. Faith in your potentials. Faith in your talents. Faith that all things work together for your good. You surround yourself with things that charge your faith. Be faith personified. Faith is the key, and the only key, to live extraordinarily in life.

Fear and faith resides in the same place in your mind. Your mind is the processing room of thoughts. Your dominant thought is what makes you. What you think about most of the time is what manifests in your life. That is why the bible says what a man thinks in his heart is who he is.

7 For as he thinketh in his heart, so is he...

Prov 23:7(KJV)

If you think that you can, then surely you will. We are all made by our dominant thoughts. All winners have always thought of winning. Who you think you are is who you are. Fill your life with thoughts of faith, possibilities, and greatness. No one can ever rise beyond his thought. Be charged with faith.

Walking on the storms of life

Faith is required to walk successfully through the storms of life. No doubt, there will always be challenges as long as you are advancing. Whether you operate in faith or fear is what determines your place in life.

Jesus commanded Peter to "Come" and walk to him on water in Matt 14:29. Peter acted in faith and "Come down out of the ship, he WALKED ON THE WATER, to go to Jesus." That is an act of faith to accomplish what naturally seems impossible.

Among all the disciples of Jesus, Peter was the only one that walked on the water because he dared, with faith, to walk on the water.

However, when Peter had walked a little, he became aware of his environment, of his circumstances, and he noticed that there is a boisterous wind, he took his eyes off Jesus. Then fear took over his faith and" he was afraid". Like many people, when starting out walking in faith and challenges comes, they begin to notice everything that is not right and become fearful.

In every challenge, there are only four possible ways to go - to go back, to stay in, to sink into or to pull through. The first three ways are the result of fear. Only men of faith pull through life challenges.

Peter became afraid and he began to sink. It is fear that sinks. Fear causes doubt. Jesus called the fearful act of being afraid by Peter as "little faith and doubt" (Matt 14:31). Doubt symbolizes little faith. Unbelief is an act of no faith.

God's system operates by faith that is why Jesus could do great and diverse miracles. That is why anointed men of God could through the power of God heal sicknesses, break shackles of devil, cast demons, and command breakthroughs.

It is faith that can take you to a greater place. It is faith that propels you to appear before kings and not before mean men. It is faith that makes you achieve what people thought is not achievable.

Walking through the storms

Something worth noting happened when Jesus and Peter got into the ship (Matt 14:32) - the wind ceased.

32 "And when they were come into the ship, the wind CEASED."

Matthew 14:32 (KJV)

Faith will pull you through the storms of life. Many people give in to fear and give up too early, when their success is near. Those challenges that seem too big are not as big as you think. The tougher it seems, the closer you are to your victory. The size of your battle determines the size of your victory. To live extraordinarily, you need faith to win extraordinarily.

It is in your darkest moment that your greatest light will shine. You have to liberate yourself from fear of the storms and challenges. You need the storms to grow stronger. The stronger the challenges you can overcome, the stronger you will be in life.

To win big in life, You will fight big.
Adefioye Sunday A

Don't give in to fear, stay and break through. The storm ceased when Jesus and Peter entered the ship.

No challenges last forever. In fact, the end of your challenges is nearer than you think. But don't give up before the time comes. Fill your life with faith and win big. It is only tough people that overcome tough times, be tough in faith - faith in God and faith in yourself. And the tough time shall never last.

Living the God's system is living in victory. Living in victory is living in faith. Living in faith is living in love.

9

LIVING THE GOD'S SYSTEM

To live the God's system, you must constantly feed your mind with thoughts of faith. Thoughts of possibilities. Thoughts of greatness. Success comes only when you operate in faith. The world system is to reduce you to nothing. But God's system is to elevate you to glory. It is faith that makes you advance in life. I have experienced fear. And I have experienced little of faith. God's system is the best. A life of faith is a life full of fun. Challenges are fun. In fact you thrive on them. Because when you operate the God's system, you are far above all principalities and challenges of life.

15 [God] disarmed the principalities and powers that were against us and made a bold display {and}public example of them, in triumphing over them in Him {and} in it [the cross].

Col 2:15(Amplified)

This does not mean challenges will not come. If you have challenge, then it means you are somebody going somewhere. Devil is not interested in non-entities, he his attracted to people of glorious destiny. And as a believer, you have a glorious destiny. But to live triumphantly on earth, operating in the God's system is essential. You should realize that you are placed with Christ far above all principalities and seated with him in heavenly places (Eph 1:20-22). And understand that you are to walk over all red seas of life on express and in peace. Awakening to the truth that you are not to fear the Pharaohs of life.

Faith exposes you. Faith redeemed you. Faith tunes you into the frequency of God. Without faith, Abraham cannot receive the blessings of God. Without faith Abraham cannot be declared righteous. Without faith, you cannot receive anything from God.

8 By faith Abraham, when he was called to go out into a place which he should after receive for an inheritance, obeyed; and he went out, not knowing whither he went.

Heb 11:8(KJV)

To live the God's system successfully, your faith must be tested. Faith is in levels. You can only grow in faith. You grow from one level to another. But you must pass the tests of your current level of faith. The advancing man knows this. He is focused on God, trusting Him in all his ways. Giving glory to Him in all situations. A man that must advance in life must know deep within his soul that whatever God has placed in his heart and has written in His Word shall come to pass. Just like Abraham who did not waver, not giving in to the world system, but kept his eyes on God's promises. And it surely came to pass.

20 He staggered not at the promise of God through unbelief; but was strong in faith, giving glory to God;
21 And being fully persuaded that, what he had promised, he was able also to perform.   *Rom 4:20-21(KJV)*

Qualification for the God's System

There are qualifications for you to live a life of victory and success. To live extraordinarily, you must operate the God's system. And to operate God's System, three steps are required.

1. Salvation
2. Baptism in the Holy Ghost, and
3. Constant feeding on God's Word

SALVATION

To advance in life, your salvation is essential. To overcome the world systems, you need to partner with someone who is greater than the world. To win in the world, you need someone who is stronger than he who lives in the world. To live and walk with peace in this turbulent and world filled with vipers and serpents, you need the prince of peace.

To exercise your power over principalities, you need the help of the one who is seated in heavenly places far above all principalities, whom has seized the keys from Hades and death.

To live in divine health, you need the one by whom stripes you are healed. To prosper in life, you need the help of the one whom by his love, though he was rich has become poor for your sakes, that by his poverty you might become rich (2Cor8:9). To advance in life, you need to accept Jesus Christ as your Lord and Saviour. He is the High priest. The one through whom we got to the Father.

6 Jesus saith unto him, I am the way, the truth, and the life: no man cometh unto the Father, but by me.

John 14:6(KJV)

To accept Jesus as your Lord and Saviour, simply confess your sins, ask for forgiveness and say the following prayers;

Dear Jesus, I believe that you are the Son of God.

I believe that you died for my sake on the cross.

I believe that my sins are forgiven and you have redeemed me from the curse of the law.

I believe that you love me.

Today ...., Lord Jesus, I accept you as my Lord and Saviour.

I surrender my life and release myself unto you.

Thank you Jesus, because I believe that you have answered my prayers.

Congratulations and welcome to a new life of peace, joy, abundance and fulfillment in Christ Jesus. In salvation, old things (sins, addictions, stagnation, joblessness, depression, poverty, sickness, diseases,, old habits, alcoholism, smoking, lust, and awkward personality) have passed away, all things are now new, and you are now a new creature in Christ. You are an ADVANCING MAN. You are moving confidently through Christ in the fulfillment of your purpose in life. You are no longer travelling your journey in life alone.

17 Therefore if any man be in Christ, he is a new creature: old things are passed away; behold, all things are become new.

2 Cor 5:17(KJV)

You are no longer a loser because you have a winner in you. You are no longer a beggar because you have direct access (through Christ) to the ultimate source of abundance in life. You have direct access to God through Christ. You can ask (according to God's will) anything you want, and believing, you shall receive.

Start to see yourself as a new creature and begin to live as the blessed because you are blessed. You are a new creature. You are a person of possibilities. You are one in Christ as Christ is one with God. You are a success. You are prosperous. You are a victor. You are healed. Glory be to God.

10

THE HOLY SPIRIT

To advance in life, and to claim your inheritance in Christ, you need a partner here on earth. Christ is seated in heavenly places, but he did not leave you comfortless. That is why he gave us the Holy Spirit.

16 And I will pray the Father, and he shall give you another Comforter , that he may abide with you forever;
17 Even the Spirit of truth; whom the world cannot receive, because it seeth him not, neither knoweth him: but ye know him; for he dwelleth with you, and shall be in you.
18 I will not leave you comfortless: I will come to you.
John 14:16-18(KJV)

26 But the Comforter , which is the Holy Ghost, whom the Father will send in my name, he shall teach you all things, and bring all things to your remembrance, whatsoever I have said unto you.

John 14:26(KJV)

The Holy Spirit is also called the Holy Ghost or the Spirit. He is the Spirit of God. He is the power of God. He is at work at creation. He is the power that raised Jesus Christ from death. He is a person. He can speak. He has emotions. He can be grieved. You can communicate with him like a friend. He is only available to work with and in you after salvation. And you receive the Holy Spirit by faith.

To advance in life, you need a helper. You need a guide. You need a mentor you can trust. This guide, this mentor, this comforter, this helper is the Holy Spirit. He is to guide you into all truth.

Right now in my office, as I am writing this book, the Holy Spirit manifested himself. He fills this office. Everywhere is charged with His power. I know he is right here, as He promised to be always with me. He lightened my spirit. I felt so alive. When the Holy Spirit manifest Himself, you can feel and sense His divine presence physically.

As a believer, the Holy Spirit is the most important friend and partner that you need. He tells you everything you need to live a fulfilled life. He warns you of impending dangers. He corrects you whenever you stumbled. He gives your life direction. The Holy Spirit is the Spirit of the Almighty God, He knows you more than you. And it is only Him that knows the heart of God. He knows the will of God for your life. As an advancing man, you need direction for your life. And Holy Spirit, the Spirit of truth, is the only partner that can give you divine direction, and guide you in the right path.

11 For what man knoweth the things of a man, save the spirit of man which is in him? even so the things of God knoweth no man, but the Spirit of God.

12 Now we have received, not the spirit of the world, but the spirit which is of God; that we might know the things that are freely given to us of God.

13 Which things also we speak, not in the words which man's wisdom teacheth, but which the Holy Ghost teacheth; comparing spiritual things with spiritual.

1 Cor 2:11-13(KJV)

The power of the Holy Spirit surpasses all human understanding, and it defiled human wisdom. You need the Holy Spirit more than money. You need Him more than food. You need Him more than your family. You need Him more than your closest friends. You need Him more than your spouse. You need Him more than your possessions. He will not leave you in trouble. He will not leave you in times of distress. He knows the end from the beginning. He knows your destiny. He knows your future. If you must advance in life, you need the fellowship of the Holy Spirit.

No prophet or pastor can give you the Holy Ghost. Nobody can give him to you. Man is only a vessel. Because he is not the Spirit of man and neither is he the spirit of the world. Only Christ can baptize you in the Holy Ghost. And once you are saved, you have access to the Holy Ghost.

16 John answered, saying unto them all, I indeed baptize you with water; but one mightier than I cometh, the latchet of whose shoes I am not worthy to unloose: he shall baptize you with the Holy Ghost and with fire:
Luke 3:16(KJV)

To receive the Holy Spirit, you develop a thirst and longing for Him. Then invite Him to be an intimate friend and a partner with you in life. Tell Him you want Him. Tell Him you need Him. Tell Him you want to fellowship with Him. Talk to Him as a friend. He understands all languages. Invite Him in your native language, invite Him in any language. Welcome Him with your heart. And believe you receive Him. Invite the Holy Spirit by saying the following prayer;

Precious Holy Spirit,
I invite you into my life today.
I want you to lead, guide and direct me.
I want to relate with you as a person.
I want to know you as a friend
I thank you for honouring my invitation,
Thank you Holy Spirit.

Believe every word of this prayer. And have faith that you received the Holy Spirit. He communicates with your spirit. He speaks to your inner man. Sometimes, you can hear him talk to you in audible voice.

The most important thing is that, you are conscious of His presence and guidance every time. His words to you can be an instant prompting, a recurrent knowing in your spirit, intuition, conscience, little unrest within you, or deep inner peace.

All these are some of the signs that the Holy Spirit is communicating with you. The Holy Spirit is a person as real as you and me.

He is the Spirit of God (not covered with flesh like we do). That is why you can only communicate with the Holy Spirit with your spirit. He has every emotion that be found in man, He can also be grieved (Eph 4:30).

When you receive the Holy Spirit, He helps you in prayer. He aids your spirit to connect with God. For God is a Spirit and anyone who worships Him must worship him in Spirit and in truth.

To effectively worship God, you need the person that knows the heart of God, who is the Spirit of truth and the Spirit of God.

Every man that advances in life and fulfilled destiny in according to the system of God has strong fellowship with the Holy Spirit.

8 But ye shall receive power, after that the Holy Ghost is come upon you: and ye shall be witnesses unto me both in Jerusalem, and in all Judaea, and in Samaria, and unto the uttermost part of the earth.

Acts 1:8(KJV)

4 And they were all filled with the Holy Ghost, and began to speak with other tongues, as the Spirit gave them utterance.   *Acts 2:4(KJV)*

Without the Holy Spirit, you have no power. You are controlled by the world's system. A life without Him is a life of defeat and desolation. It is a life with no direction; a life of no purpose; a life of weakness. Jesus Christ commanded the disciples, that they should NOT leave Jerusalem, until they receive the Holy Ghost.

4 And, being assembled together with them, commanded them that they should not depart from Jerusalem , but wait for the promise of the Father, which, saith he, ye have heard of me.
5 For John truly baptized with water; but ye shall be baptized with the Holy Ghost not many days hence.
                                          Acts 1:4-5(KJV)

Until Christ was filled with the Holy Ghost, He was not tempted (Luke 3:22). He overcame temptation because of the power of Holy Ghost in Him and He was led by the Spirit into the wilderness (Luke 4:1). And when He returned in the power of the (Holy) Spirit, He became famous throughout that region. He was empowered by the Holy Spirit to fearlessly declare His divine mandate (Luke 4:14) and to fulfill His purpose here on earth. To fulfill your purpose in life, you need the Holy Spirit. And Glory Be to God, you have him. You received Him by faith. Halleluiah!

14 And Jesus returned in the power of the Spirit into Galilee: and there went out a fame of him through all the region round about.   *Luke 4:14(KJV)*

Jesus's Divine Mandate
18 The Spirit of the Lord is upon me, because he hath anointed me to preach the gospel to the poor; he hath sent me to heal the brokenhearted, to preach deliverance to the captives, and recovering of sight to the blind, to set at liberty them that are bruised,

19 To preach the acceptable year of the Lord.

Luke 4:18-19(KJV)

One of the evidences that you receive the Holy Spirit is speaking in new tongues when you pray. As a natural man, we don't know how to pray or what to pray for, but it is the Spirit that helps us in prayer and makes intercession for us.

26 Likewise the Spirit also helpeth our infirmities: for we know not what we should pray for as we ought: but the Spirit itself maketh intercession for us with groanings which cannot be uttered.
27 And he that searcheth the hearts knoweth what is the mind of the Spirit, because he maketh intercession for the saints according to the will of God.

Rom 8:26-27(KJV)

Speaking in tongues is also known as praying in the Holy Spirit. It is communicating with God in an heavenly language. It is when you can communicate in the heavenly language that you have power to grow spiritually. The deeper you are and the more attune you are to the voice and communication in the spirit, the more powerful you will be on earth. Speaking with tongues is the evidence.

6 And when Paul had laid his hands upon them, the Holy Ghost came on them; and they spake with tongues, and prophesied.   *Acts 19:6(KJV)*

Nobody advances in life without power. I believe you receive power. Now pray in power, pray to God with your spirit. Release yourself as the Holy Spirit gave you utterance, open your heart unto him, loosen your lips and let your mouth speaks whatever words and utterance is released into your spirit. Speak it, you don't have to understand what you are saying but in your spirit, you will know that you are connected to God and His presence is real.

You are empowered, you have authority, you have confidence and you have power to advance in life and to fulfill your purpose. I congratulate you once again. You are elevated above the world's system. You are attuned to God.

11

THE WORD OF GOD

As a man of purpose, a man of vision, and a man of power, you feed on the Word of God. Your mind cannot be neutral. It is either filled with spiritual virtues or filled with worldly decadence. And remember, you are made by what you constantly feed your mind with. Jesus told the tempter that "man shall not live by bread alone, but by every word of God." Bread does not mean food only, it means all worldly desires.

4 But he answered and said, It is written, Man shall not live by bread alone, but by every word that proceedeth out of the mouth of God.

Matt 4:4(KJV)

The one who overcomes the world is the one that is filled with the word of God. You cannot have faith by feeding your mind with fear. And nobody ever succeed by feeding his mind with defeat. Whatever you feed your mind with is what manifests in your life. To operate in the system of God, you must constantly be renewed and updated in His word. His word is His will; His word is His instructions for you on earth. You seal your inheritance in Christ and advance in life by the quality of the word of God you have in you. The system of God operates on faith. And faith comes by hearing the word of God. Faith comes by feeding on the word of God.

17 So then faith cometh by hearing, and hearing by the word of God.

Rom 10:17(KJV)

You hear the word of God by attending a bible-based church, reading anointed books, listening to anointed messages and music, watching anointed movies, and keeping quality and faith-filled friends.

The only thing that God required of Joshua to prosper and succeed in his mission in life is to

(1) ceaselessly speaks the word of God

(2) meditate in the word both day and night (every time), and

(3) to believe and do everything that is written in it

And only when these requirements are met, can his way be prosperous and have good success.

8 This book of the law shall not depart out of thy mouth; but thou shalt meditate therein day and night, that thou mayest observe to do according to all that is written therein: for then thou shalt make thy way prosperous, and then thou shalt have good success.

Josh 1:8(KJV)

To advance in life and to overcome life struggles, you must be addicted to the word of God. You must be soaked in it. When you are saturated in God's word, you operate in the supernatural. Your faith is extraordinary.

Your level of understanding in the word of God and how much Word you have in you, determines the level of breakthrough that you command in life. You only understand what you feed in your mind and meditate upon. You can only benefit from what you put into practice.

Caleb could not see the giants and he knew that the Israelites are more able to possess the land (Num 13:30). He charged a whole nation because he was a man with understanding in God's word. Many people went through life as grasshoppers while they see life challenges as giants. The God's system is the only way to lasting victory in life. And the manual for the system is God's word.

To advance and overcome life challenges, spend quality time in the Word of God. The Word is God Himself speaking to you. There can be no creation without the Word (John 1:3). In the account of creation as written in Chapter One of Genesis, the Spirit of God was upon the face of the waters in a formless and chaotic world - and nothing happened until God spoke.

It is the power of the Holy Spirit and the Word of God that creates changes and brings about supernatural results. To effect changes in life, you need to be strong in the Word of God. Jesus was filled with the Holy Spirit and led by him into the wilderness to be tempted (Matt 4:1) but he would not have overcome the tempter without the Word of God. God's word is His command and you command life situations using God's Word.

You need to immerse yourself in the Word of God to create the changes you desire in life. The Word of God is the light that gives you understanding and wisdom to use the power of God in you to show forth His praises and to command excellence in life.

You are only approved of God by how well you study, meditate and act on His word.

15 Study to shew thyself approved unto God, a workman that needeth not to be ashamed, rightly dividing the word of truth. *2 Tim 2:15(KJV)*

By constant study of the Word of God, you are renewing your spirit man, feeding him with spiritual food (the Word). Each time you study and meditate on God's word, you receive new revelation and inspiration.

You are strengthened in the Lord and empowered to challenge the Pharaohs of life, to command breakthroughs and to do exploits. That is why when Jesus told Simon (Peter) to cast his net into the sea (Luke 5:5), when Peter complied he said "nevertheless AT THY WORD I will let down the net". And at the Lord's word" they inclosed a great multitude of fishes: AND THEIR NET BRAKE". In verse 7 of that Luke 5, Peter began to summon his partners to help him pack the fishes, they came and also fill their boats. Something happened, "they began to sink" (Luke 5:7). You need the word of God to command a net breaking victory and breakthroughs. To advance in life you need His Word.

2 *"And be not conformed to this world: but be ye transformed by the renewing of your mind, that ye may prove what is that good, and acceptable , and perfect, will of God."*   *Rom 12:2 (KJV)*

When you are filled and constantly renewed in the Word, you operated in a realm beyond the retarded and unstable system of the world. You are divinely instructed and guided. You know what is right and good. According to that Roman 12:2, renewing your mind will enable you to prove what is good, what is acceptable, and perfect will of God. Since the will of God is His Word which is written by the inspiration of His Spirit, you can only know the (good, acceptable and perfect) will of God by studying and meditating in His word.

With the Holy Spirit, you have power (Acts 1:8) and with the Word you have authority. The word of God is called the "Sword of the Spirit" in Eph 6:17, and sword is a symbol of authority. You have authority both in the spiritual and in the physical.

17 "And take the helmet of salvation, and the sword of the Spirit, which is the word of God:"   *Eph 6:17 (KJV)*

To advance in life, you need to be saved, fellowship with the Holy Spirit, and constant feeding on the Word of God. This is what makes you qualify to live and walk in victory in every facet of life.

12

YOU CAN HAVE ALL YOU NEED IN LIFE

As an advancing man who is saved, have the Holy Spirit and is growing in the Word of God. Your advancement and the level of your breakthroughs is a function of making your desires become realities and in fulfilling your purpose according to the will of God. Every purpose in life is composed of needs, wants and desires. The accumulated manifestation of these needs and desires is what brings meaning to life.

You are only advancing when your needs are met and your desires becomes reality. And Glory be to God, because you can have all your needs met and you can transform all your desires into realities. Every person that advances in life knows this quite well.

To have everything you want in life requires four steps. With these four steps, you can have everything you want in life according to the will of God.

You can transform your life into wonders. You live a life filled with testimonies. You live a life of accomplishment. The required steps to have everything you need to advance in life are given by Christ in Matthew 21:22;

22 *And all things, whatsoever ye shall ask in prayer, believing, ye shall receive.*

Matt 21:22(KJV)

It is written in Matthew 21:22 that AND ALL THING, not some things. All things and it also says WHATSOEVER. Whatsoever means anything and everything regardless of size, quantity or weight. No specification. The limit of whatsoever is determined by the limit set by the person concerned or the object of interest. Combination of all things and whatsoever means imaginable and beyond.

And the all things and whatsoever is first CONCEIVED IN THE MIND. The second step to having everything that you need is to ASK. And you ask in prayer. The third step is to BELIEVE. And the fourth is to RECEIVE. The four steps are to;

1. CONCEIVE/IMAGINE
2. ASK
3. BELIEVE, and
4. RECEIVE

Step 1: CONCEIVE/IMAGINE

6 And the LORD said, Behold, the people is one, and they have all one language; and this they begin to do: and now nothing will be restrained from them, which they have imagined to do.   Gen 11:6(KJV)

Without a vision, there is no purpose. Without a purpose, there is no will. Without a will there is no advancement in life. Clearly define your vision and purpose.

You define your vision and purpose by first conceiving them in your mind, you visualize them in your imagination. Imagination is the creation of images in your mind. The stronger the essence of the image you hold in your mind, the greater the assurance of its manifestation.

When the people of the old testament gather together to build the tower of Babel, God says that nothing that they have put their mind into shall be withheld from them, everything they have imagined and believe they can do, they will do.

The pictures that you hold in your mind, sooner or later manifest in its physical form. The mind is the linking room to the supernatural. Everything that you can see in the world today begins as a small idea or simple imagination in the mind of someone. The aircrafts, rockets, communication gadgets, large ships, speeding boats, exotic cars, mansions, and all the inventions are all a seed of thought before they were transformed into their physical equivalent. These illustrate the power of vivid conception of what you really want in life in your mind. You first see it in your mind. You create it in the spiritual.

You decide and conceive what you really want. The size and quantity does not matter. The same way a pencil is first conceived in the mind of someone, so is the super computer and a whole mega city conceived in the mind of someone, both are made of the same substance and materials in the spiritual (mind). They are created by the same amount of energy - thought. That is why the bible warns in the book of Proverbs that you should guide and keep your heart with all diligence, might and effort because every issue in life proceeds and are created out of it (the emphasis is mine).

23 Keep thy heart with all diligence; for out of it are the issues of life   Prov 4:23(KJV)

The same way wealth is created so is poverty created. The seeds that you conceive and sow in your heart determine the fruits that manifests in the physical. Imagination is the seed of greatness.

All the great men that the world has ever produced are men of great imaginations. They conceive great ideas in their mind. And since the bible says, whatsoever you have imagined to do you can achieve, the things you conceive in your mind are essentially the determinant of the things that manifest in your life.

Some people manifest abundance, others manifest lack. Some manifest wealth and other manifest poverty. Some manifest divine health, others manifest sickness and diseases. Some manifest multiple job opportunities, others manifest joblessness and underemployment. What are you conceiving in your mind? Fill your mind with positive thoughts based on the Word of God.

Conception is the first step to getting all you need in life. Every man that advances in life knows this. Everyone who has achieved great results in life understands this. To advance in life, you must begin to conceive those things that you want in your life. You must begin to create them in your mind.

Jesus says in Matt 21:22 that "all things and whatsoever", and God says in Gen 11:6 that "nothing will be restrained from them, which they have imagined to do". The first step to getting everything that you need in life is to conceive and imagine those things and whatsoever that you want in your mind.

Step 2:   ASK

7 Ask, and it shall be given you; seek, and ye shall find; knock, and it shall be opened unto you:
8 For every one that asketh receiveth; and he that seeketh findeth; and to him that knocketh it shall be opened.
Matt 7:7-8(KJV)

The second step to have your needs met in life is to ask. And you ask according to the will of God. What you don't ask you cannot receive. It is only when you ask that you have something to receive.

23 For verily I say unto you, That whosoever shall say unto this mountain, Be thou removed, and be thou cast into the sea; and shall not doubt in his heart, but shall believe that those things which he saith shall come to pass; he shall have whatsoever he saith.

Mark 11:23(KJV)

Ask is the same as "saying" as Jesus Christ told us in Mark 11:23. The mountain can be anything in life. It can be mountain of debt, mountain of failure, illness, stagnation, frustration, anxiety, worry, or any other challenges of life.

How do you ask? You ask in prayer. You ask when you set goals and make plans. You ask by repeatedly saying it within your heart and confessing it loudly and openly with your mouth.

To advance in life, you know that you must have a purpose. To fulfill your purpose require asking in prayer, making plans and setting goals.

Goal setters are go getters. The go-getters are the pace setters. The world is filled with exceptional pace setters. The geniuses in technology, science, engineering, research, etc. People working to make the world a better place, they are pace setters. And largest numbers of them are goal setters.

When you have a goal and it is written, almost half of the goal is settled. When you need a thing and you ask, you have successfully increased your chances of getting it above 50%. But when you don't ask you have 0% chances of getting what you want.

Asking opens the doors and the channels through which your request will be granted and those things you have conceived come to pass. When you ask you have successfully initiated a spiritual process to bring your request to reality. It is only by asking that things manifest here on earth. Even the whole world was created by a process that starts with "saying" or asking. God speaks the word and everything in it into being.

1 In the beginning was the Word, and the Word was with God, and the Word was God.

2 The same was in the beginning with God.

3 All things were made by him; and without him was not anything made that was made.

John 1:1-3(KJV)

You are a supernatural being, made in the image of God. God says "let there be light" before there was light (Gen 1:3). And Jesus says "...whosoever shall say unto this mountain..." (Mark 11:23).

Advancing man knows how to ask their heavenly father the desires of their heart. And they also know how to speak to mountains on their paths. They know the right Words to say to every mountain because; they have good knowledge of God's Word. Jesus Christ did not conquer the devil by manly, worldly speeches, or an eloquent oratory. He conquered the devil (tempter) by the Word of God. And he advances in his earthly ministry because of the Word in him.

If you must advance you must ask what you have conceived in your heart. You must speak what you know is truth every time.

When you ask in prayer, you are establishing your desires in the spiritual. You are writing a request in your file in heaven. You inform God about your desires. You activate the heavenly process to bring your desires (things conceived in the mind) to manifestation.

When you ask in written form, setting goals and making plans, you are initiating earthly process for bringing your desires to manifestation. You are creating the physical form of what you impress upon the supernatural. You are establishing a footprint for bringing what you desire into manifestation.

And the Lord answered me, and said, Write the vision, and make it plain upon tables, that he may run that readeth it.   Habakuk 2:2

The plans you make after prayers are not ordinary. They are delivered to you by God as the channel through which your request will be granted. Sometimes, when you conceive something's in your mind, and you pray about it, you receive some ideas about how to transform what you have in your mind into its physical equivalent.

Planning gives you direction to the insights and ideas to get what you ask. It serves as the link between you and your desires. Prayer answers all things. When you pray and ask, whatever you ask is established with God. The plan and idea that you received after you ask is your guide for the manifestation of your desires. No greatness is accidental.

Asking is the next step after you have conceived in your mind what you really want for you to advance in life. In whatever you want in life, new job, healing, business breakthrough, freedom from debt, deliverance, life partner, etc. To effectively ask your desires in prayer, write it down on a clean sheet of paper, then present it to God and pray about it. Then put down the ideas, insights and plans you receive during or after prayer. That is your road map.

Step 3: BELIEVE

Many great visions have died simply because of lack of believe. If you don't believe in your vision, nobody will believe in it. If you don't believe in yourself, nobody will believe in you.

Believe is the greatest factor that determines whether what you ask for shall manifest (is realized) or not.

When you ask, what you ask is established. But it is your believe that will make what you ask manifests. Your ideas, insights and plans can only work if you believe in them. Nobody has ever received anything he does not believe. The advancing man's believe is powered by faith.

When you believe, you have an understanding that what you ask will manifest. But when your believe is charged by faith, then you have an understanding that you receive what you ask. Believe alone cannot make your desire to manifest, is has to be mixed and powered with faith. That is why in the amplified version of that Mark 11:23 says that "... having faith {and} [really] believing..."

22 And whatever you ask for in prayer, having faith {and}[really] believing, you will receive.
Matt 21:22(Amplified)

You have to believe that you receive what you ask and not that you will receive. When you believe without faith, you believe you will receive. But when your believe is charged by faith, you believe that you receive. Believing without faith is an expression of future manifestation of what you ask. And believing with faith is an expression that what you asked for is manifest.

You believe with your heart and you know very well within your soul that you have what you ask. When you truly believe with faith, it affects your emotions, your speech, appearance and thought. With true believe, you will have peace and joy from within signifying the manifestation of what you ask.

The power behind every one that advances in life is faith and believe. When you strongly believe in what you want, it will surely manifest.

Step 4: RECEIVE

Receive is the actual manifestation of what you have conceived in your mind and see clearly in your imagination; asked for in prayer; and have believed.

Sometimes if your believe and faith is so strong, when your desire finally manifest, you may not notice instantly, because you are already living it, all your emotions are already in it, you have synchronize yourself with it without any worry or anxiety. Just as Jesus did not take note of the fig tree, he doesn't have to worry or be anxious whether what he has said will come to pass.

The sweetest part of life is when you have all you need in life. This is the type of life that God want you to live. A King does not lack anything in his kingdom. And remember, you are a chosen generation, a royal priesthood . . . (1 peter 2:9).

9 But ye are a chosen generation , a royal priesthood, an holy nation, a peculiar people; that ye should shew forth the praises of him who hath called you out of darkness into his marvelous light:

1 Peter 2:9(KJV)

It is your responsibility to show forth the praises of God. It is your responsibility to reign as king on earth. It is your responsibility to live in dominion.

10 And hast made us unto our God kings and priests: and we shall reign on the earth.

Rev 5:10(KJV)

GRATITUDE

God wants you to advance in life. God wants you to reign in life. You must always acknowledge him in everything you do and every situation you are. Always be grateful to him and be thankful to him. Gratitude is an essential factor that will determine how far you advance in life and how often you have your needs met. Before what you want manifest, be grateful that you receive because you asked. When it manifests be grateful that you receive. Be grateful everyday of your life. Be grateful in every moment. Jesus fed five thousand with the power of gratitude (Mark 8:6, Matt 15:36). He was grateful for what he has and he received what he wants. Gratitude will transform your life in big ways.

When you are grateful for small things you open the door for bigger ones. Gratitude makes your believe and faith effective. Gratitude will propel your advancement in life. Always find something to be grateful for in every situation.

As an advancing man, you have all you need in life in Christ Jesus. You are advancing in life because you are empowered by God and you have the Holy Spirit. You know that your eternal source of everything is God. And you know that everything always works out for your good. Now arise, get up and refuse to be pitied, advance confidently to the fulfillment of your destiny.

1 Arise, shine; for thy light is come, and the glory of the LORD is risen upon thee.
2 For, behold, the darkness shall cover the earth, and gross darkness the people: but the LORD shall arise upon thee, and his glory shall be seen upon thee.
3 And the Gentiles shall come to thy light, and kings to the brightness of thy rising.

4 Lift up thine eyes round about, and see: all they gather themselves together, they come to thee: thy sons shall come from far, and thy daughters shall be nursed at thy side.

5 Then thou shalt see, and flow together, and thine heart shall fear, and be enlarged; because the abundance of the sea shall be converted unto thee, the forces of the Gentiles shall come unto thee.

Isa 60:1-5(KJV)

You are a rising star. You are a wonder to behold. You are advancing in life. You are growing in power. You are moving to the next level. You are moving ahead. You are living in abundance. You are living in dominion. You are blessed. And you are a blessing. In Jesus Name. Amen!

EPILOGUE

You have successfully completed this book.

I congratulate you as a winner, a victor and an advancing man and woman.

This book contains practical biblical guides for living a life of victory and advancing confidently in the fulfillment of destiny. It contains steps that help you overcome the world's frustration and confusion. The principles and concepts presented serves as light to help you live according to the truth in God's Word. To live abundantly and victorious. Remember, Godly faith work by love. As you advance in life, spread love and be a blessing.

This is a transformational book which have both inspires and motivates you. Put everything in it into practical use. Like every other principles, they work when they are worked.

Be blessed and be a blessing. Keep advancing!

- ADEFIOYE SUNDAY ADEWUMI

NOTES

NOTES

NOTES

ABOUT THE AUTHOR

Adefioye Sunday Adewumi is Word of Faith Bible Institute Graduate - the leadership development arm of the Living Faith Church Worldwide.

He is an author, inspirational speaker and a published independent researcher.

TO CONTACT THE AUTHOR

Please include your testimony or help received from this book when you write. Your prayer requests are also welcome.

Adefioye Sunday Adewumi
Sadaxx Systems
Ile Ife,
Osun State,
Nigeria.

Hotline:
Tel: (+234) 703-3985-337,
       (+234) 818-6948-268
Email: sunday.adefioye@gmail.com

Follow us on Facebook:

http://www.facebook.com/TheAdvancingMan

www.ingramcontent.com/pod-product-compliance
Lightning Source LLC
Chambersburg PA
CBHW070302230426
43664CB00014B/2616